THE SCHOOL OF LIFE is dedicated to exploring life's big questions: *How can we fulfil our potential? Can work be inspiring? Why does community matter? Can relationships last a lifetime?* We don't have all the answers, but we will direct you towards a variety of useful ideas – from philosophy to literature, psychology to the visual arts – that are guaranteed to stimulate, provoke, nourish and console.

About the Cover Image: The cover of this book features the Danish North Sea, to represent the home and birthplace of Kierkegaard

By the same author:

The Hammer and the Cross: A New History of the ...
Henrik Ibsen: A New Biography
Enigma: The Life of Knut Hamsun
The Short Life of T.E. Hulme

By Søren Kierkegaard:

Either/Or
Fear and Trembling
Repetition
Three Discourses on Imagined Occasions
Concluding Unscientific Postscript to Philosophical Crumbs
Two Ages: A Literary Review
The Lily in the Field and the Bird of the Air
The Sickness unto Death
Papers and Journals

≈

First published 2013 by Macmillan
an imprint of Pan Macmillan, a division of Macmillan Publishers Limited

Pan Macmillan, 20 New Wharf Road, London N1 9RR
Basingstoke and Oxford
Associated companies throughout the world
www.panmacmillan.com

ISBN 978-1-4472-4564-3

Cover designed by Marcia Mihotich
Cover image © Corey Arnold
Typeset by seagulls.net
Printed and bound by CPI Group (UK) Ltd, Croydon, CR0 4YY

LIFE

LESSONS

FROM

KIERKEGAARD

ROBERT

FERGUSON

MACMILLAN

Søren's father Michael was from the lowest peasant class. In 1777, at the age of twenty-one, he was released from service by his master and within a short space of time had made a fortune as an importer of textiles. By the time he was forty he was rich enough to retire. Søren was born when he was fifty-six, the child of his second marriage to Ane, his former housekeeper. Michael Kierkegaard was a deeply religious man. There is a story that as a boy of fourteen, out tending his master's sheep, he had cursed God for the unfairness of his fate, and the subsequent dramatic change in his fortunes following the outburst seems to have haunted him with guilt. He instructed Søren in a dark vision of Christianity that Søren resented for a long time, feeling he had had no real childhood at all. Later he learned to see the legacy as a chance to reinvent his own idea of what being a Christian really meant. With his father's death in 1838 Søren inherited a fortune that relieved him of the need to earn a living and enabled him to start in earnest on what he had decided would be his life's work: as a thinker and writer.

At the heart of Kierkegaard's life and thought lies a most remarkable love story. In May 1837, at the house of a Copenhagen friend, he met and subsequently pursued the precocious and talented Regine Olsen. In 1840, when she was eighteen years old, he proposed to her and was accepted. In September 1841 he broke off the engagement, and shortly afterwards published the book that made him famous throughout Scandinavia and that is probably still the title most commonly associated with his name, *Either/Or*.

Like almost all the products of Kierkegaard's prodigious literary activity, *Either/Or* was published under a pseudonym. Written in a variety of contrasting voices and styles, the book's most famous or notorious section is 'A Seducer's Diary', an account by a young man named Johannes of the incredible lengths he goes to in order to win the love of a young woman. Success, as it turns out, is the object of the whole exercise; having won her heart he then ends the relationship, leaving himself free to seek out another target for his diverting campaign of conquest.

Just exactly *why* Kierkegaard broke with Regine is one of the great enigmas of his life. It is clear from his subsequent writing, and particularly the *Journals and Papers*, that he continued to love her, so much so that on his death in 1855 he bequeathed what small amount of money he had left to her, explaining that he did so because he regarded their engagement as being the same as a marriage. She, however, had long since married someone else and the bequest was declined.

In *Either/Or* Kierkegaard presents his readers with a division of life into three 'stages on life's way' (actually four, though the first is never referred to as a stage), each constituting an advance on the one before it: the philistine, the aesthetic, the ethical and the religious.

Though he used pseudonyms to write 'in the voices' of people at all of these stages (showing a notable affinity with those at the 'aesthetic stage'), in his own view he was always a religious writer, concerned to persuade his readers of their absolute need to take the philistine–aesthetic–ethical–religious path to Christ. His commitment to something as 'irrational' as Christianity has led many philosophers to dismiss him as not a 'proper' philosopher at all, and he was well aware that many found his position intellectually dubious. Yet one of the most stimulating paradoxes about Kierkegaard is that, with all his love of Christ, his was also one of the most rational, intellectual, analytically precise and psychologically acute minds most of us are ever likely to encounter. For me, reading him is like going on a long walk in the company of a fascinating companion. Much of what he says is too abstruse and complicated, even too personal, for me to understand; much, much more of it is enlightening, profound, thought-provoking and enriching. As an agnostic I cannot follow Kierkegaard all the way to the gates of the heaven he sees so clearly in front of him, and we always part company before he reaches his final destination. But from my point of view at least, it is far more fun to travel interestingly than to arrive.

One of the ideas most commonly associated with Kierkegaard is that a 'leap of faith' is required in order to understand and accept the shattering significance of the New Testament story and the assertion of the divinity of Christ. Again, it is difficult to know whether one has understood exactly what he meant by this, but it seems to me that he is referring to the idea that a rational approach to knowledge will always, in the end, come up against limits, but that a thousand subjective impulses continue to whisper to us that these limits are not the end at all. And is his idea of the 'leap of faith' really so strikingly irrational? Every child, on first hearing that the universe began in a 'Big Bang', immediately wants to know *what came before that?* Science's best answer is that a 'Singularity' existed, meaning a state in which the known laws and understandings of our science simply do not apply. Kierkegaard's 'leap of faith' is no less unnatural a response than that to the ultimate question of just exactly who – or what – is running the restaurant at the end of the universe.

Kierkegaard's health was never good. When he was out walking one day his legs collapsed beneath him. He was able to make his way to Frederiks Hospital in Copenhagen and have himself admitted. From the start he appears to have regarded the illness as fatal and over the next eight weeks his bodily functions gradually broke down. Just prior to his collapse he had launched an extraordinary attack on the Lutheran Church in Denmark, accusing its priests and bishops of being not much more than a religious bureaucracy interested largely in making people – themselves included – comfortable. He died on 11 November 1855, just forty-two years old. The doctor who treated him in his final illness wrote the one-word question 'Consumption?' on the front of his Patient's Journal, but the exact cause of death remains a matter of debate.

1

HOW TO WAKE UP

....

> The most important thing is that a person should grow in the soil to which he really belongs; although where that might be is not always easy to know. In that respect there are certain lucky souls who have such a clear bias in one particular direction that, once it has been pointed out to them, they head straight off in that direction and are never troubled by the possibility that, in fact, they should really have been taking a completely different path. And then there are others, so completely conditioned in their progress by their immediate surroundings that they never fully understand what it is they really should be aiming for.
>
> (*Papers and Journals 1833–1855*,
> published posthumously)

There is really just one thing Kierkegaard wants us to understand, and that is that most of us are sleepwalking our way through life. Functioning sleepwalkers, to be sure. Some of us might be important men and women in the world; we might be captaining industry, running economies, even running countries. But worldly success means nothing if we are still asleep, sleep-walking our way through a life we never asked for and a world we built as a response. He suggests there are very good reasons why we don't want to open our eyes, not the least of which is how frightening and disorientating it might be to wake up one day to the true confusion and despair from which sleep has shielded us:

> You stick your finger into the ground to smell what country you're in. I stick my finger into existence – and there's no smell at all. Where am I? What is that supposed to mean – in the world? What does the word mean? Who has lured me into all this and then left me standing here? Who am I? How did I get into the world? Why was I never asked? Why was I not taught the rules and customs here but just stuck into the ranks as though I'd been bought from some travelling slave-trader? How come I am a participant in this huge enterprise known as Reality? Why should I be a participant? Is there no choice in the matter? And if there is no choice, then where is the manager – there's something I want to say to him. Is there no manager? Then to whom shall I address my complaint?
>
> (*Repetition*, 1843)

Kierkegaard devotes a lot of time to this state of affairs we find ourselves in:

Of all ridiculous things, it seems to me what is most ridiculous is to be busy in this world, to be a man who hastens to his food and hastens to his work. That is why, when at some critical moment I see a fly land on the nose of one of these businessmen, or he gets soaked by some carriage driving by in even greater haste than his own, or he has to wait while the river bridge goes up in front of him, or a tile falls from the roof and kills him, I laugh heartily. Who, after all, could fail to laugh? What is it, actually, that they achieve, these furiously busy people? Is there any difference between them and the woman who, in her confusion when a fire broke out in the house, salvaged the fire-tongs? Do they really salvage anything more from the great confla-gration of life?

(*Either/Or*, 1843)

Kierkegaard can seem cruel and off-putting in his desire to tell his truth. A good marriage? Forget it – it's all part of the great circus of self-deception:

The dangerous thing about being married is all the hypocrisy involved, that one does what one does for the sake of the wife and children. One sinks into worldliness and cowardice and then puts a sanctimonious gloss on the whole thing – it's really very good of you after all, because the whole thing is being done for the sake of the wife and children.

(*Papers and Journals 1833–1855,*
published posthumously)

We might even toss the book away and say we'll go elsewhere if we want to be insulted. But then he takes pity on us and gives us a clue as to why he is engaging in all this mockery, what it is that bothers him so and what he knows, deep down, bothers us too – if only we would acknowledge it:

Ultimately, what is the purpose of this life? If we divide mankind into two large groups we might say that the one works in order to live while the other has no need to. But surely working for a living can't be the meaning of life. Surely it is self-contradictory to say that this – the constant effort to provide the conditions of living – should be an answer to the question of the purpose of life, since living itself is what creates those selfsame conditions. Nor, generally speaking, do the lives of the other class have any purpose beyond consuming the conditions of living. To maintain that the purpose of life is to die seems like another contradiction.

(*Either/Or,* 1843)

This is why he wants to help us, because he knows that every last one of us has these moments in which we doubt that the whole thing has any meaning at all. But just as quickly he's back prodding us again. He's particularly fond of paradox as a way of trying to wake us up and keep our attention as we come to understand that his cruelty and wit are directed as much against himself as against the rest of us:

If anybody keeps a diary it should be me, to help jog my memory a bit. I often find myself completely forgetting what it was that moved me to do this or that thing, go to this or that place, and not just in trivial matters but in matters of real moment. And if I then do happen to recall the reason, it sometimes strikes me as so strange that I refuse to believe it. If I had written notes on which to rely then doubts like this would be wholly removed. A reason is actually a very strange thing altogether: if I endow it with all the passion at my disposal then it swells until it becomes a consuming necessity, capable of moving both heaven and earth; but if passion is absent then I look down upon it. For some time now I have been wondering what it was that caused me to leave my post as a secondary school teacher. Looking back, a post like that was the very thing for me. And today it dawned on me that this was precisely the reason – that I had regarded myself as ideally suited to the position. Had I carried on in my post I would have had everything to lose and nothing to gain. So for this

> reason it seemed proper to relinquish the post and take employment with a travelling theatre company, since I had no talent for such work and therefore everything to gain.
>
> (*Either/Or*, 1843)

With increasing severity he warns us that boredom is the most sinister and destructive of all enemies, driving us to fill our days with activity as we try to make life seem meaningful and important. It could, of course, be very boring to hold forth at length about being boring, but Kierkegaard found a solution to this – he did so with humour:

> People who know about such things assert that starting from a basic principle is a very sensible way to proceed; so I'll defer to them and start from the basic principle that all people are boring. Or will someone be boring enough to contradict me over this? . . . Everyone who has dealt with children will acknowledge just how corrupting boredom is. As long as children are enjoying themselves they are always good. This is true in the most literal sense, because if they sometimes become difficult even while playing, the real reason is that they have begun to bore themselves.
>
> (*Either/Or*, 1843)

He makes what he claims is therefore an obvious point – that the ability to amuse children is as important a quality in a nursemaid as those other, more conventionally prized virtues such as sobriety, trustworthiness and decency. Still teasing, still forcing us to stay awake, to pay attention, he heightens the level of absurdities:

> but so remarkable are the ways of the world, so greatly have habit and boredom taken over, that the case of the nanny is the only one in which the claim of aesthetics is properly honoured. A person who files for divorce on the grounds that his wife is boring, or who demands that a king be dethroned because he is so boring to look at, or a priest driven into exile because he is so boring to listen to, or a Cabinet Minister dismissed or a journalist given a life sentence because they are so outrageously boring, will get nowhere with his demands.
>
> (*Either/Or*, 1843)

In fact, Kierkegaard shows us as readers a great deal of respect for our intelligence by using the sophisticated codes of irony and hyperbole to uncover the fact that, in the lives most of us lead, we are each a part of a crowd of self-validating sleepwalkers. There are solutions – there must be, otherwise what would be the point of waking up? Kierkegaard would be better to let sleeping dogs lie. The solution he proposes in the first instance is a simple and attractive one: that, waking up to the essential absurdity of life, we look on it as a game, and play it with a serious creativity that should do a great deal to dispense with this problem of boredom. He takes a final swipe at the still-sleeping –

> So all people are boring ... The word 'boring' itself can as easily refer to someone who bores others as to someone who bores himself. Those who bore others are the crowd, the mass, the common run of humanity in general. Those who bore themselves are the few, the elite; and the wonder of it is this, that those who do not bore themselves generally bore others, while those who do bore themselves amuse others. Those who do not bore themselves are generally speaking the industrious people of the world, which is precisely why these are the most boring and most intolerable of all.
>
> (*Either/Or*, 1843)

– before going on to propose a solution:

> The secret of the whole thing lies in being arbitrary. People suppose that there is no special art to being arbitrary, and yet it is a profound study to be arbitrary in such a way that one does not get lost in the process but is able to derive pleasure from it. One does not enjoy the immediate object of one's pleasure

but something else, another element which one has arbitrarily introduced. One sees the middle of a play, one reads the third part of a book. In this fashion one derives a quite different enjoyment than that which the author has so kindly intended for us. One enjoys something entirely accidental, one contemplates the whole of existence from this standpoint and allows reality to run aground there. Let me give an example. There was a man whose chatter the circumstances of my life obliged me to listen to. For every occasion he had some small philosophical lecture ready to hand, excruciating in its boredom. On the very brink of despair I noticed suddenly that he perspired to a quite unusual degree while lecturing. I now concentrated my attention on this perspiring. I observed how the beads of sweat gathered on his forehead, how they combined into a rivulet which then trickled down his nose and gathered as a large drop on the very tip of it. From that moment on everything changed. On occasion I even actively encouraged him to embark on one of these improving lectures of his, solely for the pleasure of tracing the trickling of that sweat from his forehead to his nose.

(*Either/Or*, 1843)

If it's funny it's also bleak. And as with all of Søren Kierkegaard, there is a 'to be continued'. His irony, his indirect method of instruction, this apparently cynical injunction to take a step back and become a cool student and an observer of life and cultivate what he called the 'aesthetic' response to life, are not the ends that they were for Oscar Wilde's aesthetes, or Huysmans's Des Esseintes. He proposes them as a means to an end that still lies a long way off. But if we can follow him this far then we have understood at least one very important thing: that we can *choose*.

2

HOW TO SEE
THROUGH THINGS

....

Our secondary schools tend not to offer classes in philosophy and so we grow up imagining it to be some kind of authoritative science of life that – if we could only understand it – would tell us exactly who we are, why we're here and where we're going. But as a glance at a single page of Bertrand Russell's *Principia Mathematica* or Wittgenstein's *Tractatus Logico-Philosophicus* will reveal to us, modern Western philosophy is an esoteric pursuit with little relevance to our actual daily lives. For the simple reason, then, that I appeared to be able to understand it, Descartes' *'Cogito ergo sum'* – 'I think, therefore I am' – acquired great importance for me as an earnestly questing young man. Pithy and absolute, it seemed to hold out the promise, with enough thinking, of vast and relieving insights into the meaning of life. For the same reasons I was greatly attracted to the Buddhist idea of *satori*, apparently a sudden blinding moment in which the shackles fall from our mind and everything becomes completely clear. After that, getting through life would be a breeze.

Well, time passed, these illuminations never dawned, and suddenly the race was on and we were all heading full speed down the tunnel of life into jobs, careers and marriage; these existential preoccupations were dismissed as adolescent luxuries as we got down to the business of living our actual and real lives. Watching us, remembering his own life, Kierkegaard immediately starts laughing:

> When I was very young and in the cave of Trophonius I forgot to laugh. Then, when I got older, when I opened my eyes and saw the real world, I began to laugh and I haven't stopped since. I saw that the meaning of life was to get a livelihood, that the goal of life was to be a High Court judge, that the bright joy of love was to marry a well-off girl, that the blessing of friendship was to help each other out of a financial tight spot, that wisdom was what the majority said it was, that passion was to give a speech, that courage was to risk being fined 10 rix-dollars, that cordiality was to say 'You're welcome' after a meal, and that the fear of God was to go to communion once a year. That's what I saw. And I laughed.
>
> (*Either/Or*, 1843)

Perhaps in due course we get the idea ourselves and we start to laugh too. Those big questions about 'the real self'? If they made a comeback at all they did so humorously. One of the American humourist Jack Handey's *Deep Thoughts* always seems to me to capture the mood of this type of humour perfectly: 'I hate to tell you this', he writes, 'but if you think a weakness can be turned into a strength, that's just another weakness.' So does a cartoon from Gary Larson's *Far Side Gallery* that shows a bespectacled badger standing in the self-help section of a bookshop engrossed in a book entitled *Dare to be Nocturnal*. Very funny comments on our absurd modern belief that there is no such thing as nature and that everything has to be taught (you can even buy books on how to *walk*) – but very much laughter in the dark, and a dead end too. In the 'Diapsalmata' section of *Either/Or* Kierkegaard tells a joke about a joke about a joke:

> At a theatre once a fire broke out backstage. The clown came on to warn the audience. The audience thought it was a joke and applauded; he repeated what he had said, and the applause increased. I think that's how the world will come to an end: to the general acclaim of witty types who think it's all a joke.
>
> (*Either/Or*, 1843)

Kierkegaard was *furiously* learned. He knew his Greek and Roman mythology and literature, his Old and New Testaments, his Old Norse mythology, his Shakespeare and his Goethe, and he was deeply read in the influential philosophers of his own era. His vast learning kept him entertained; but it was a substitute, its very vastness a desperate tactic to conceal a deeper sense of emptiness, and he knew it:

> I stand here like a man who has rented an apartment and bought furniture, and yet still has not found the beloved with whom to share the ups and downs of his life. But diving ever deeper into the world is not the way to find 'the great idea' or, more accurately, to find my true self. That is precisely the way I tried to do it before. That is why it seemed such a good plan at the time to begin my legal studies, as a way of developing my expertise in the face of life's many confusions. Because here I encountered a wealth of individual cases in which to immerse myself. Here I might, from the available facts, construct a totality, an organism of criminal life which I might follow in all its darker aspect (here too a certain spirit of association seems noticeably present). That is why I wished to be an actor, so that by thinking myself into the role of another I might acquire, so to speak, a surrogate for my own life, deriving some pleasure from this outward exchange. That was what I was lacking in order to lead a completely human life and not simply a life of knowledge, so that I did not base the development of my thought on – well, on something

people call objectivity – on something that, whatever else it might be, was not my own; but instead on something that connects to the deepest root of my existence and through which I, so to speak, grow into the divine and become one with it, even if the whole world should fall apart. See, that is what I lack, and that is what I am striving for. That is why with a joy and an inner strength I consider those great men who search for that precious gem for which they would sell everything, even their lives; whether I see them intervening decisively in life, striding firmly, not wobbling, as they follow their chosen path; or encounter them on some remote byway, absorbed within themselves as they work towards the lofty goal. I honour even those wrong trails that lie in such close proximity to these others. What matters are a person's inner actions, his God-side, not a great mass of learning.

(*Papers and Journals 1833–1855*,
published posthumously)

So what should we do, if all our learning turns out to be nothing more than a diversion, a way of passing the time? If we find out that instead of being ourselves we have become actors, playing the part of ourselves? We can laugh, of course. Humour is one way of masking the pain of existential emptiness, and when I finally began reading Kierkegaard seriously it was a pleasure to discover how funny he could be. The 'Diapsalmata' section of *Either/Or* contains this despairingly hilarious protest against the horrors of having to choose:

> Marry, you'll regret it; don't marry, you'll regret that too; marry or don't marry, you'll regret it either way; whether you marry or you don't marry, either way, you'll regret it. Laugh at the world's follies, you'll regret it; weep over them, you'll regret that too; laugh at the world's follies or weep over them, you'll regret it either way; whether you laugh at the world's follies or weep over them, either way, you'll regret it. Believe a girl, you'll regret it; don't believe her, you'll regret that too; believe a girl or don't believe her, you'll regret it either way; whether you believe a girl or don't believe her, either way, you'll regret it. Hang yourself, you'll regret it; don't hang yourself, you'll regret that too; hang yourself or don't hang yourself, you'll regret it either way; whether you hang yourself or you don't hang yourself, either way, you'll regret it. This, gentlemen, is the essence of all life's wisdom.
>
> (*Either/Or*, 1843)

Bracing in its absurdity, Kierkegaard's over-the-top rant makes us realize that he is defying us to take him seriously. Again, it's laughter in the dark and he is hinting at the urgent need to do something more than just laugh.

Though he trained as a priest Kierkegaard did not believe in the value of direct sermonizing. Instead he promoted through his writing what he called 'indirect communication', in which what we learn from his descriptions of his passage through life comes to illumine our own journey. An early reader of *Either/ Or* wrote to his mother of how 'exceedingly offensive' he had always found Kierkegaard, 'from the very first time I made his acquaintance'; but that on reading the book the reason for his hatred had become clear to him: 'this singular personality is my own caricature'. Many readers since have seen their own caricature in a passage like this:

> How lovely it is to be in love, how interesting it is to know that one is in love . . . And should I not feel easy in the mind, I who can consider himself favoured of the gods in being granted the rare pleasure of falling in love yet again? No art, no study can produce the thing, it is a gift. But once I have been fortunate enough to stir up erotic love again, then I am curious to see how long it can be sustained. I cosset this love in a way I never did the first one. Experience shows that these episodes are few and far between, so it is beholden on one to exploit them, because the real frustration is that while there is no problem in seducing a girl, it is rare pleasure indeed to find a girl who is worth seducing. – Love has many mysteries,

and this first falling in love is one, though among the lesser of them. Most people rush ahead and get engaged, or do something else equally stupid, and in a trice it's all over, and they have no idea of what it is they have gained nor what they have lost.

(*Either/Or*, 1843)

Over and over again Kierkegaard describes his aesthetes, his ironic and detached observers of others, manipulators like the seducer Johannes, with an accuracy and an irony so cold that we cannot possibly want to be like them. Kierkegaard knew that, like Walt Whitman, he contained multitudes, which is one reason he wrote under so many pseudonyms. Unlike Whitman, however, the insight made him uneasy. He wrote about the numerous possible selves we contain, the repertoire we command as actors, the options we acquire by taking a step back from life, to fall in love with love, and do it over and over again, hiding from ourselves the fact that this is what we are doing – for if we could, with Johannes, say how beautiful, how *interesting* it is to be in love, the knowing would put an end to the fun, the game would be over, and we would be as disappointed as children being shown the secret of the conjuror's tricks.

We have found a seemingly inexhaustible source of self-stimulation to ward off the most terrible disease of all that comes with the realization that we are never going to find *satori*, never going to leap from our baths with a great cry of joy as the full meaning of *cogito ergo sum* finally dawns on us: existential boredom. As the narrator of *The Seducer's Diary* puts it: 'I fear neither comic nor tragic predicaments; the only ones I fear are the boring ones.' The whole of *The Seducer's Diary* is dedicated to exposing this type of personality, and in so doing urging us, if we recognize our caricature here, to wake up to the fact and see through this false self. What is thrilling about Kierkegaard is that, his task of revelation completed, he does not smugly retire with a smile on his face. He does not give up. Leaving behind the aesthetic response, he continues his search for meaning and urges us to do the same. He feels certain that the emptiness we have been working so energetically to avoid might not, in fact, be an emptiness at all.

3

HOW TO AVOID
LIVING IN THE PAST

....

One of the great myths of rationalism is that there is a trick or a knack to being happy, and that if only we could learn this trick we should be happy for the rest of our lives. Publishers make fortunes from books that promote the idea. The trouble is that our happiness seems to be as arbitrary and illogical as the weather. We really don't know why happiness suddenly manifests itself, and we don't know why it as suddenly disappears either. With typical irony Kierkegaard gives a personal account of his own experience of the sensation of passing happiness in a passage in *Repetition*:

> Anyone who has given the matter any serious thought will know that I am right when I say that it is never given a person to be absolutely and in every conceivable way completely content, not even for one single half-hour of his life. I hardly need add that for such a state of affairs to arise something more than sufficient food and clothing is required. I did come close to it once. I rose one morning feeling quite

unusually well; in defiance of all previous experience this sense of well-being increased as the morning advanced; at precisely one o'clock I reached a peak, a dizzying maximum previously unrecorded on any known barometer of well-being, not even on the thermometer of poetry. My body felt weightless, as though I had no body, precisely because every function savoured its own complete satisfaction, every nerve delighted in itself and in the whole, every beat of my pulse and all of the inner restlessness only memorialized and defined the joy of the moment. My walk was a soaring, not like the flight of a bird that cuts through the air and leaves the earth but like the billowing of wind over a field of corn, like the longing rocking of the sea, like the dreaming drifting of the clouds. My being was as transparent as the depths of the ocean, as the self-satisfied silence of the night, as the silent monologue of the midday. Within my soul each mood rested in melodic resonance. Every thought was open to me, each one inviting, with the same joyous exuberance, the silliest whims as well as the greatest profundities. I sensed the coming of each new impression even before it arrived and awoke inside me. All of existence seemed to be in love with me, everything moving in a preordained rapport with my being; all was prescient in me, all riddles resolved in a microcosmic bliss in which all was explained, even what was most disagreeable:

the dullest remark, the most repulsive sight, the most calamitous conflict. As noted, it was at precisely one o'clock I reached a peak and had intimations of the most exalted of all when, suddenly, I got something in my eye, an eyelash or a speck of dust, something or other, I don't know what it was. What I do know is that at that selfsame instant I plummeted to the depths of despair – easy enough to understand for anyone who has been up as high as I was, and even at that precise moment preoccupied with the theoretical question of the degree to which it is possible to attain absolute and complete contentment. Since then I have abandoned hope of ever knowing complete and universal contentment. I have abandoned even the hope I once entertained of knowing, if not complete contentment at all times then in isolated moments, even if, as Shakespeare says, 'A tapster's arithmetic may soon bring his particulars therein to a total.'

(*Repetition*, 1843)

Probably not as often as we would like, we all have moments of extended bliss like this. And of course, Kierkegaard doesn't expect us to feel sorry for him once his hour has passed. But rather than this spontaneous manifestation of happiness he wants us to consider our response to another, very different experience of happiness; the remembered happiness of times past, when we think we know *why* we were happy and make a deliberate attempt to regain that happiness by recreating the circumstances of that previous occasion.

Often this will be because we're unhappy with the circumstances of our present lives. We didn't get the job we wanted; our marriage isn't working out; we're struggling to pay our bills; we're getting old and our health is breaking down – or it might be because we're unhappy or embarrassed or guilty about something we did in the past, the way we treated someone, and wish we could go back in time and change things. All his life Kierkegaard wrestled with the idea that he had treated his young fiancée Regine Olsen badly, and his struggles gave him a peculiarly acute insight into the futility of believing that to go back is a real option for any of us. Even if we make the most careful and scrupulous attempt to recreate the physical conditions associated with a time of happiness in the past – the same house, the same street, the same face at the window – it won't work. Here he describes a trip he made to Berlin in order to try to relive former pleasures:

> After having concerned myself for some length of time, at least when the opportunity presented itself, with the problem of whether or not a repetition is possible, and whether something is improved or made worse by being repeated, it suddenly occurred to me: But of course – you can go to Berlin, where

you were once before, and find out there whether repetition is possible, and what the significance of it might be.

. . .

I want to talk briefly about a voyage of discovery I made to investigate the possibility and potential significance of repetition. Without informing anyone of my plan (and thereby avoiding a lot of chatter that might have invalidated the experiment and in various other ways made the idea of repetition boring) I travelled by steamship to Stralsund and booked a seat on the express mail coach to Berlin. There is scholarly disagreement over which is the most comfortable seat on a coach. My view is as follows: all of them are unspeakable. On the previous occasion I had had one of the outer seats towards the front (in the view of some a great advantage) and for the next thirty-six hours was so comprehensibly shaken together with my neighbours that by the time I arrived in Hamburg I had lost possession not only of my reason but of my legs as well. During the hours that the six of us spent in that coach we were so thoroughly shaken together that we dissolved into a single body, and I was reminded of those simple-minded inhabitants of the town of Molbo who had spent so much time sitting together that in the end they were unable to recognize which were their own legs. This time, in the hope of being a limb on what would at least be a smaller body, I chose a seat in the coupé. That made a change. But still, everything repeated itself. The postilion blew his horn, I closed my eyes and spoke to myself, as I usually do on such occasions: God knows if you'll survive this, if you'll really get to Berlin, and if you do whether you'll ever be a human being again and capable of liberating yourself in the individualism of isolation, or whether this memory of being a limb on a huge body will always be with you.

And yet I did get to Berlin.

Straight away I hurried off to my old lodgings to settle this matter of whether a repetition was possible.

(*Repetition*, 1843)

The first disappointing departure from the script is that his landlord has now married and is using the room he formerly rented, obliging him to make do with a different room. In order to heighten the chance of repetition displaying itself to him he goes to the theatre to attend the performance of a play with which he is already familiar. This looks promising. And yet, as he discovers, sometimes the repetition you get is not the one you wanted:

Der Talismann was to be performed at the Königstädter Theatre. The memory of it awoke in my soul and I saw it all so clearly, just as it had been on that former occasion. I hurried off to the theatre. This time there were no individual boxes to be had . . . and I found myself among a group of people who were uncertain whether to be entertained or bored – the kind one can with complete certainty dismiss as boring . . . I stood it for half an hour and then left the theatre, saying to myself: naturally, there is no such thing as repetition . . . I headed off to the cafe which I had frequented each day on my previous visit . . . Perhaps the coffee would be as good as it was last time. One might almost assume it would be. And yet it wasn't to my taste.

In the evening I went out to the restaurant I had frequented on my previous visit, and where, presumably from force of habit, I had even enjoyed myself. Having gone there each evening I was familiar with every detail of the place. I knew when the early visitors left, the particular fashion in which they said goodbye to those remaining behind, whether they put their hats on in the inner room or the outer room, or not until they'd opened the door, or not until they were outside. No one escaped my notice; like Proserpine I plucked a hair from every head, even from the bald. It was the same in every respect. Same jokes, same little courtesies, same mild inebriation, the whole place just the same – in short, a sameness within a sameness. Solomon says that the quarrelling of a woman is like a dripping from the roof – who knows how he would have reacted to this still life! Appalling thought, but repetition was indeed possible here.

I was at the Königstädter Theatre again the next evening. The only thing that repeated itself was the impossibility of a repetition. No matter which way I turned, all was in vain. The little dancer who had enchanted me on the previous occasion with a grace that seemed poised to leap had now done her leap; the blind man in front of the Brandenburg Gate, my harpist – I was probably the only one who was concerned about him – was now wearing a greyish coat instead of the light green one that I longed to see in my melancholy, the one that made him look like a weeping willow. He was lost to me.

. . . When all this had repeated itself for several days I became so embittered and bored with repetition that I decided to go back home. What I had learned was remarkable, although not significant. I had discovered that there is no repetition, and I had made absolutely certain of the truth of this by having it repeated to me many times, in numerous different ways.

I vested all my hopes in home. Justinus Kerner tells a story somewhere about a man who grew bored with his home and had his horse saddled up with the intention of riding off into the wide world. After he had ridden a short distance the horse threw him. It turned out to be a decisive moment for him, for as he turned to remount his gaze once more fell on the home that he was so keen to leave. He looked and he saw that it was so lovely that he at once returned. In my own home I felt tolerably certain I would find everything poised for repetition. I have always been deeply suspicious of all upheaval, even to the extent of hating every form of cleaning, and above all the scrubbing of floors. I had accordingly given the strictest instructions that my conservative principles be respected also during my absence.

But what happens? My faithful servant was of another opinion. He presumed that in beginning a ferocious cleaning very shortly after my departure all would be over by the time I returned, confident in his own ability to put everything neatly back just the way it had been. I arrive, I ring on my own door-bell, my servant opens the door. It was a remarkable moment. My servant turned as pale as a corpse as, through the half-opened door, I beheld the appalling sight: everything was upside down. I was stunned. In his bewilderment he had no idea what to do and as his guilty conscience overcame him he slammed the door in my face. This was too much. With my need now at its greatest height my principles wilted and I feared the worst . . . I understood that there really is no repetition, and that my former understanding of life had triumphed . . .

Time passed, my servant made amends for his earlier wrong, and a monotonous uniformity once more descended upon my affairs. Whatever couldn't move stood in its ordained place, and whatever could, moved in its predictable course: my clock, my servant – and myself, pacing up and down across the floor. For even though I had ascertained that there is no repetition, it will always be the case that inflexibility and a sort of wilful dulling of one's powers of observation will produce a uniformity that is far more stupefying than the most whimsical of diversions, and that in the course of a lifetime will grow ever stronger, like an enchantment.

(*Repetition*, 1843)

Kierkegaard often reminds us of the dangers of trying to control life too much, to escape its vagaries and surprises by turning it into a trustworthy and unchanging routine. With an eye to the theatricality of the Danish postal service he offers a personal and beguilingly surreal solution to the whole problem:

Hail the post horn! For many reasons, that is the instrument for me. And most particularly for this reason, that one can never be completely sure of coaxing the same note from it twice. There are endless possibilities in a post horn, and whoever puts it to his lips and applies his wisdom to it will never find himself guilty of a repetition, and whoever instead of answering a friend presents him with a post horn for his pleasurable convenience says nothing but explains everything. Praise be to the post horn! That is my crest. As the ascetics of old placed a skull on the desk and devoted their lives to meditating upon it, so shall the post horn on my desk always remind me of what the meaning of life is. Hail the post horn! But the journey is not worth the inconvenience suffered, for one scarcely need move from the spot to be persuaded that there is no repetition. No, one sits quietly in one's room, when all is vanity and has passed away, and yet journeys more swiftly than one does on a train, despite the fact that one is sitting quite still. Everything shall remind me of this. My servant shall wear the livery of the postal service, and when dining out my only conveyance shall be the post-chaise. Farewell, farewell, rich hope of youth! Why all this haste? That which you chase does not exist, no more than you yourself do! Farewell, manly strength! Why do you tramp so hard on the ground? That which you tread upon is an illusion! Farewell, triumphant resolve, you will not reach your goal, for you cannot take your deed with you unless you turn back, and that you cannot do. Farewell, beauties of the forest, already faded by the time I wanted to see you! Roll on, you fleeting river, the only thing that really knows what it wants, that wants only to run and lose itself in the sea, which will never be filled! Play on, you drama of life, which none call a comedy and none a tragedy, because none have seen how it ends! Hurry along, you drama of existence, where life does not come back any more than money spent does. Why has no one ever returned from the dead? Because life does not know how to fascinate as death does, because life cannot persuade the way death does. Yes, death is a matchless persuader, provided one does not attempt to contradict it but lets it talk on. Its persuasion is instantaneous, so that none have ever raised a word in objection, nor longed to hear the persuasion of life.

(*Repetition*, 1843)

Kierkegaard's idea of 'repetition' is actually more than a simple rejection of the desire to live in the past, either by indulging an addiction to memory or by the actual physical recreation of a set of once-familiar circumstances. He uses the term in a special philosophical sense to mean that if we simply put our trust in the unfolding moment of life (or in God's infinite repertoire of possibilities), then there is no need ever to prefer the past; the most unexpected things may well happen to us just a few seconds from now.

4

WHY WE SHOULD
CULTIVATE DISSATISFACTION

....

Most of us assume that a feeling of dissatisfaction, with our lives or with ourselves, is a bad thing. After all, it feels uncomfortable. Kierkegaard had no interest in comfort (at least, not in intellectual or moral comfort; he was fond enough of the physical comforts afforded him by his inherited fortune). He believed it was natural for our mental life to be difficult and uncomfortable, and that these challenges were even good for us. With his religious upbringing it was natural for him to use the Bible as a kind of sourcebook for every conceivable kind of existential question that life might present us with. This also had the advantage of making him access-ible to a wide contemporary readership, through the shared frame of reference which the Bible was at that time. In his native Denmark he became very angry at the way priests somehow contrived to make reading the Bible a risk-free undertaking. He was determined to make people take their intellectual and moral lives seriously, to be fearless in making things difficult for themselves. It's another of his ways of getting us to wake up, of reminding us to question the credentials of the professional wise men and women amongst us, be they priests or psychoanalysts. *Don't just accept the experts – challenge them:*

There is a wisdom which would presume to introduce into the world of the spirit the same law of indifference under which the physical world labours. It holds that it is enough to know the great truths – no further work is required. For this reason it gets no bread and dies of hunger while all around it turns to gold. And what does it know, really? In the time of the ancient Greeks there were many thousands, and thousands more in later generations, who knew all of Miltiades' triumphs, but only one was rendered sleepless by them. Countless generations have known the story of Abraham word for word, off by heart: how many has it made sleepless?

The story of Abraham has this strange quality, that it will always be glorious, no matter how impoverished the understanding of it, provided that here, too, people are willing to 'labour and be heavy laden'. But they don't want to work, and yet still they want to understand the story. One speaks in honour of Abraham, but how? By casting the whole story in an everyday form: 'This was what was glorious, that he loved God so greatly he was prepared to sacrifice the best he had to him.' That is certainly true; but 'the best' is not a precise term. In the normal run of thought and speech one can safely identify Isaac and 'the best', and with that the thinking man can puff away on his pipe as he thinks, and the listening man stretch out his legs comfortably in front of him as he listens. If the rich young man whom Christ met along the way had sold his property and given away the proceeds to the poor we should certainly praise him highly and have to work at understanding him; and yet still he would not be an Abraham, in spite of his offering the best he had. What gets left out of the story of Abraham is the anguish; after all, I am under no ethical obligation to my money, but a father is under the highest and holiest obligation towards his son. But then anguish is a dangerous area for the squeamish, so we leave it out; and yet still we wish to talk about Abraham. And so we talk, and in the course of our speech we make the two interchangeable, Isaac and the best, and it all works out most satisfactorily.

But if just one among the listeners in church happened to have stayed awake during all this then an awful and tragicomic misunderstanding lies dangerously close at hand. He goes home. He wants to emulate Abraham. And his son is the best he has. If the preacher should learn of what has happened, then he might go to him, and with all his priestly dignity rage at him: 'Loathsome person! Outcast among men! What devil possessed you that you should murder your own son!' When he delivered his sermon about Abraham the preacher had noticed no signs of sweating or flushing, but now he astounds himself with the passion of his seriousness as he thunders at the poor man. He feels proud of himself. Never before has he spoken with such fervour, such passion. To himself – and to his wife – he says: 'I am an orator. All I lacked was the opportunity to show it. In the sermon on Sunday, when I spoke of Abraham, I didn't feel anything in particular at all.' If that same speaker had even a slight surplus of wit still left to lose he might well lose it then should the sinner quietly and with dignity reply: 'It was only what you yourself preached on Sunday.' How could a priest get it into his head to do something like that? And yet his only mistake was not to know what he was saying. How astonishing that no poet has written about a situation like this instead of all the trivial nonsense with which our comedies and novels are stuffed! Here the comic and the tragic entangle in absolute infinity.

How is one to explain a paradox like that illumin-ated by our speaker? Is it because Abraham has, by the simple repetition of tradition, become such a great man that whatever he does must by defi-nition be great, but that when anyone else does the same then it's a sin, a sin to high heaven? If that is the case then I do not want to be any part of such a thoughtless chorus of praise. If faith cannot make it a holy act to murder one's son, then let Abraham be condemned in the same way as anyone else.

(Fear and Trembling, 1843)

Kierkegaard gets to the heart of the matter here – the importance of fearless thinking for anyone who is interested in *really* getting to the heart of a matter – even if it leads us to a degree of sleeplessness and dissatisfaction with the received truths:

If it appears that one lacks the courage to think the thought all the way through and call Abraham a murderer, then it would probably be better to acquire that courage rather than waste time making speeches in undeserved praise of him. The ethical expression for what Abraham was doing is that he was about to murder Isaac; the religious, that he was preparing to sacrifice Isaac. The anguish that arises when confronted by such a dilemma would be enough to make anyone lose sleep; and yet without that anguish, Abraham is not Abraham. Or perhaps Abraham did not do what the story says he did; perhaps by the standards of those times what he did was something completely different, in which case let us forget about him, for of what use is it to remember a past which cannot also be a present?

... If one removes the element of faith by reducing it to insignificance, what remains of the story is simply that Abraham was prepared to murder Isaac and that, for anyone without faith – that is to say, the faith that would make doing such a thing so hard – copying him would be an easy enough matter.

For my part I do not lack the courage to think a thought all the way through and thus far I have encountered no thought that I have feared. Should I do so, then I hope that at the very least I shall have the honesty to say: 'This thought frightens me, it stirs up something inside me and I will not think it.'

(*Fear and Trembling*, 1843)

Here Kierkegaard is addressing a common fear, that we should find ourselves censoring our own thoughts. The simple fact that he is able to identify the danger like this inclines one to suppose that Kierkegaard would never, in fact, do as he feared and avoid an uncomfortable or difficult thought. The example of his courage here is a useful lesson for us to bear in mind as we go through life, with any luck at least half awake.

5

ON NOT THINKING
TOO MUCH

....

When the Levite passed by that unfortunate man who had been attacked by robbers on the road from Jericho to Jerusalem it may well have occurred to him, while he was still some distance away, that it would be a beautiful thing to help a man who was suffering. He might even have thought how rewarding the good deed would be in itself, and perhaps, being immersed in his thought, slowed down a little. But the closer he approached, the more apparent the difficulties became, and so he rode on. Riding faster now, to get away from the thought of how dangerous the road was, away from the possibility that the robbers might be close by, and away from the thought of how easily the victim might confuse him with the robbers who had left him lying there. And so he did nothing.

(*Concluding Unscientific Postscript to Philosophical Crumbs*, 1846)

We can all think of situations when we've reasoned our way out of a dilemma or shirked a task or obligation for what we decide afterwards were very good logical reasons. We manage to ignore the sneaking feeling that all we've actually done is make a respectable-seeming excuse not to do something we were simply afraid of doing – either because we were afraid to fail, or because we were afraid to stand out from the crowd. Kierkegaard's essay *The Present Age* is a critique of this kind of culpable passivity. The 'present age' he was writing about was the 1840s, but in fact the sort of dilemmas he sketched are true of almost any age:

> Ours is essentially a common-sense, reflective age, passionless, briefly flaring up in moments of enthusiasm and then wisely reverting to indolence ... Nowadays not even a suicide kills himself in desperation. He thinks about it so carefully and for so long that the thinking chokes him, so that it's doubtful whether one can even call him a suicide at all, since it was actually the thinking that killed him. He dies not *with* deliberation but *from* deliberation.
>
> (*Two Ages: A Literary Review*, 1846)

He even sees in his own times something that looks very much like a foreshadowing of our own consumer society, in which we are in constant danger of being pacified by television, by so-called 'compassion fatigue', so seduced by the quality of the illusions created by our digital media that the lives we are living are almost virtual lives:

> By contrast with the action of a revolutionary age, ours is an age of advertisement and publicity. Anything at all that happens is at once broadcast and reported upon. A revolution now would be the last thing imaginable; any such powerful expression would appear ridiculous to the calculating common sense of our age.
>
> *(Two Ages: A Literary Review*, 1846)

Kierkegaard goes to great lengths to expose the ways in which we organize our lives so as to make them safe and comfortable on a daily basis. Of course, there's really nothing wrong in wanting to look after yourself and live as long and as comfortably as possible. What he objects to is the dishonest way in which we *elevate* the next-best things into the best and most hazardous things, so that we can applaud ourselves and approve of ourselves, creating a myth of our own qualities that works because we are all agreed in subscribing to it:

> Suppose that the treasure everyone longed to possess lay far out upon a layer of ice so thin that death itself kept watch over it, ensuring that it was mortally dangerous to make any attempt to go that far out, and that (let us allow this peculiar fact which

is, after all, only peculiar as an image) closer to land, the ice was frozen solid and much safer. In a passionate age the crowd would cheer the brave man who dared go out so far; it would tremble with him and for him in those decisive moments when his life was at risk; it would grieve for him in the hour of his failure, and worship him should he win the treasure. Matters would be very different in a passionless and reflective age. Everyone would sensibly agree with everyone else that the only sensible thing to do was not to go out that far, and indeed that to do so would be rash to the point of foolishness. In so doing they reduce a feat of enthusiasm and daring to nothing more than a display of skill – in order to at least do *something*, 'because *something* must be done'. So the crowd will assemble out there and, from some secure vantage point, coolly savour the efforts of the skilful skaters as they show their ability to approach as close as possible to the danger area (i.e. to a point at which the ice was still safe and danger not yet present) before turning back. Among the skaters there will be the occasional outstanding talent, someone so skilled that even while at the outermost limits he is able to make yet another disappointed effort to complete the task, with the crowd crying out: 'Oh God, he's mad, he's risking his life.' But look – he was so skilled that, after all, he was able to turn back just in time, where the ice was still safe, and danger not yet present. Precisely as in the theatre the crowd would cry bravo and shower him with praise, and return home with the great hero-artist in their midst, there to honour him with a sumptuous banquet. So completely had common sense taken over that it had transformed the great task into an artistic achievement, and turned reality into a theatre. At the banquet that evening the admiration would reach its height.

Now the true conditions of admiration are these: that the admirer is edified by the thought that he, too, is human, like the object of his admiration; and while humbled by the thought of being unable to accomplish the great deed himself he is able to take moral encouragement from the hero's example to do what he can to the best of his ability. Common sense alters these conditions. Even at the height of the celebrations the admiring guests would have a shrewd idea that the honoured hero among them really wasn't all that unusual, and that it was actually quite arbitrary who they celebrated, since any of those present could, with a little practice in the art of *only just failing*, have done the same thing. Briefly, instead of being edified in their discernment and encouraged to do good, the guest would more likely return home with an increased disposition to that most dangerous, if also most refined, of all diseases – to admire in public what one privately finds insignificant – since the whole thing has become a joke, and the secret understanding behind the bells and whistles of admiration is that one might just as well be admiring oneself.

(*Two Ages: A Literary Review*, 1846)

We're all prone to this kind of response, keen to be praised, keen to think highly of ourselves. Kierkegaard, who lived a pretty sedentary life himself, was, despite his choice of the skater as an example, thinking of a lack of moral and intellectual courage. It's as though we all agreed to find Hamlet extraordinary even if he didn't, in the end, overcome his thinking and avenge the murder of his father. Kierkegaard calls the essential hypocrisy of agreeing to admire someone for doing very little 'the most dangerous' symptom of this 'disease', but we might also recognize ourselves in the slightly different sort of response he analyses, which occurs when this corporate hypocrisy either isn't in place, or isn't functioning efficiently enough. This is a general-ized feeling of envy and resentment about life:

Just as in a passionate age enthusiasm is the unifying principle, so in a passionless and over-reflective age envy becomes the negatively unifying principle. This should not be understood as an ethical charge, because the idea of reflection is – if one can put it this way – envy. A twofold form of envy, in which the selfishness within the individual himself generates selfishness in society's attitude towards him.

(*Two Ages: A Literary Review*, 1846)

He returns here to one of his central passions, the importance of being true to yourself and what you believe, and of sticking to that belief even if it makes you unpopular – either because of the nature of what you believe, or because those around you resent you for having the courage to think an independent thought:

The envy aroused by reflection in the individual renders him unable to take a decision subjectively. And if it looks as though he might be on the point of successfully doing so then the opposition of the reflection surrounding him prevents it. The envy implicit in reflection traps the will and the strength inside a sort of prison. The individual must first break free from the prison in which his own reflection detains him; and even when he has done this he is still not free but remains a prisoner inside the larger confinement created by the reflection in those around him, to which he is compelled, by the operation of the reflection within himself, to relate . . . With all the means at its disposal, reflection works to obscure the fact that it is reflection itself – and not tyrants, nor the secret police, nor priests, nor yet aristocrats – which imprisons both the individual and the age, and to preserve the flattering delusion that the possibility of reflection is greatly superior to a straightforward decision. The demands made upon the individual by selfish envy are so great that they prevent him from doing anything.

. . . But the more this goes on the clearer it is that the envy in reflection turns into envy at an ethical level. Trapped air always turns poisonous, and in the same way reflection that is trapped and ventilated by neither action nor incident turns into a damning envy . . . So the more reflection takes over and becomes inaction, the more dangerous does envy become, because it does not have the character to be aware of what it actually is. This lack of character makes it cowardly and inconstant, so that it inter-prets the same thing in a variety of different ways, all according to the dictates of circumstance. It will try to make a joke of it, and if this fails then it will characterize it as an insult. And if this in turn fails then it will dismiss it as of no importance at all. Or it will treat the whole thing as a witticism, and if this doesn't work either it will deny it was meant that way, and claim instead that what makes it worthy of attention is that it was intended as an ethical satire; failing this, it will conclude that the whole thing was of no importance at all and that nobody need pay any attention to it.

(*Two Ages: A Literary Review*, 1846)

He wants to ensure that we preserve the best and bravest that is in us, and that if we have standards of belief and behaviour we should try to adhere to them – every moment of every hour of every day of every year. Most of us, however, would probably settle for something like 'considerably more often than not'. He describes a street fight he once saw as an illustration of how contagious bad behaviour can be, and how its temptations are never greater than when we find ourselves in a crowd that is turning into a mob:

> I once witnessed a brawl in which three men shamefully set about a fourth. The crowd stood watching in indignation. The growing murmur of disapproval presently leads to action: a couple of men grab hold of one of the attackers and knock him to the ground etc. etc. So the avengers made use of the same rule as the attackers. If I might be allowed to intrude my own person into the narrative here – I stepped forward and tried to point out to one of the avengers the logical inconsistency of this conduct; but it was apparently impossible for him to concede the point, for his only response was repeatedly to claim that 'it serves him right, the rascal, if he's got three men against him'.
>
> (*Two Ages: A Literary Review*, 1846)

Kierkegaard can become so involved in his conversation with his own several selves that at times it's like trying to follow a tennis match involving five players. You don't know where to pay attention any more; the simple pendulum of eyes left-right-left-right goes haywire. Fortunately he occasionally stops to provide a brief and devastatingly clear statement of the essence of what he's trying to say. He does so in this essay too:

> Reflection is not the evil. The evil is the state of reflection, and the stasis that comes with reflection. These are corrupting and dangerous because, by conceding the possibility of withdrawal, they make retreat an easier option.
>
> (*Two Ages: A Literary Review*, 1846)

6

WHEN TO SAY NOTHING

....

One of Jack Handey's *Deep Thoughts* goes like this: 'If trees screamed, could we still chop them down? Yes, if they screamed all the time, for no reason.' Kierkegaard, in his less surreal fashion, also wrote about the benefits and drawbacks of our ability to communicate pain and suffering.

The world we live in now, the Digital Age, the Communications Age or whatever label the future will decide to give it, is really not all that different from the one in which he lived. His time seemed to him as wordy and as full of randomly used language as ours does to us, with our social media, our tweets, our seemingly endless array of devices intended to stave off the horrors of boredom, even while walking down the street or riding on a bus. The whole idea seems to be that, at any given moment, something *better* and more *interesting* is always happening somewhere else and not, almost by definition, where we happen to be. 'Nothing ever happens but there is immediate publicity everywhere,' as Kierkegaard wrote in *The Present Age*.

There is tremendous pressure to join this cacophony of digital sound and wind; we may even start to worry that we're being judged as people by the amount of noise we make ourselves, whether in a crowd at the pub, or on Facebook. It's easy to fall into the trap of believing that unless we're constantly emitting some kind of noise then we don't really exist.

And yet we know that all of this noise is not really communicating anything. It's another aspect of our culture of rationalism, the belief that we should express everything. Increasingly, towards the end of his short life, Kierkegaard came to distrust speech and 'self-expression', and to believe that a certain kind of silence was the ideal way to get through life. In a discourse entitled *The Lily in the Field and the Bird of the Air* he tries to explain why:

How solemn they are out there, under God's sky, the lily and the bird. And why? Ask the poet; he answers: 'Because there is silence there.' And he yearns to be part of that solemn silence, away from the worldliness of humans, where there is so much talking, away from that whole worldly life of being human which offers only speech as pitiful evidence of human superiority to animals. 'Although what kind of superiority is that really,' the poet will continue. 'No, I greatly prefer the silence out there. I prefer it, there's no comparison at all. The silence is infinitely superior to the world of humans, with all their speech.' Naturally, in the silence of nature the poet supposes that he senses the voice of the divine; not only does he not sense the divine in the busy speech of humans, he does not even feel the sense of a human connection to the divine. The poet says: speech is the advantage the human has over the animal, true enough – if the human knows how to be silent.

And that is something that can be learned out there, from the lily and the bird, where there is silence, and where there is something divine in that silence. Silence is out there, and not only when all falls silent in the silent night but also through all the day; when a thousand strings are in vibration and all things are as though a sea of sound, there is still silence out there. Every small part of it, and all the great totality of it, observes it so well that nothing breaks the solemn silence. Out there is silence. The forest is silent. Even when it whispers it is silent. For even in its densest parts the trees do what humans seldom do, in spite of their promises – they keep their word to each other: this will remain between us. The sea is silent, even when it rages and boils it is silent. In the beginning perhaps you do not hear it properly, what you hear is the raging. If you hurry on and take this impression with you then you do the sea an injustice; but if you linger and listen more attentively then you hear – how remarkable! – you hear silence. For what is uniform is often also silence. When evening silence rests over the land, and from some far meadow you hear the lowing of cattle, or from a distant farmer's house the homely bark of the dog, then neither this lowing nor this barking disturb the silence. No, this is part of the silence, in a secret pact with it, deepening it.

So let us then look more closely at the lily and the bird, from whom we are to learn. The bird is silent and waits: it knows or, more accurately, it has complete faith that all things happen at their appointed hour, and that is why it waits. Yet it knows that it cannot know the hour or the day, and that is why it is silent. It will happen when the time comes, says the bird, although no, the bird doesn't say that, it is silent. But its silence is eloquent, and what its silence says is that it believes, and because it believes it falls silent and waits. And when the moment comes then the silent bird understands that the moment has come. It uses it and is never disappointed. The same is true of the lily, it is silent and waits. It does not ask impatiently: 'When will the spring come?', knowing that it will come when the time is right, knowing how little it would be to its advantage were it able to decide the coming of the seasons on its own account. It doesn't ask: 'When are we going to get some rain?' or 'When is the sun going to shine?' or say: 'Now it has rained too much' or 'Now the sun is too hot.' It doesn't try to find out in advance what the summer is going to be like this year, how long or how short – no, it is silent and waits, in all its simplicity; and yet it is never deceived, for only the smart can be deceived, not the simple, who neither deceive nor can be deceived. Then the moment arrives, and when the moment arrives the silent lily understands and uses it. Oh, you deep-minded masters of simplicity, is it not possible to experience such 'moments' when speaking? No, the moment can only be experienced in silence. By the very act of speaking, uttering just a single word, the moment is missed. The moment exists only in silence. That's why a person so rarely understands when the moment has come, and how to use the moment, because he is unable to be silent. He cannot be silent and wait, that must surely be the explanation why the moment never came for him; he cannot be silent, which must surely explain why he did not notice the moment when it came for him. For the moment, with all its rich cargo of meaning, sends no advance warning of its arrival; it comes too quickly for that and there is no prior moment in which to warn of its coming. Nor does the moment, no matter how profound, come in a blare of noise. It comes softly, its footfall lighter than anything in creation, with all the stealth of immediacy. So complete silence is necessary if one is to sense its presence: 'Now it is here.' And the next moment it is gone, which is why absolute silence is necessary if one is to succeed in using it. Everything depends on 'the moment'. And this is the tragedy of so many lives, that they never sensed 'the moment', and that in their lives the eternal and the temporal were always separate. And why? Because they could not be silent.

(*The Lily in the Field and the Bird of the Air*, 1849)

Kierkegaard's thoughts on silence praise it both as conducive to a meditative ecstasy and as the best response to suffering. It feels natural for us to voice our complaint when things go wrong for some reason, but Kierkegaard suggests that, in fact, talking about our trials and troubles probably magnifies them and makes them worse rather than better. Again he urges us to consider the possibility that a stoical response resembling that of the bird and the lily means our troubles will never seem greater than they are, and that with any luck they will disappear in the natural flow of time without any interference from us:

The bird falls silent and suffers. No matter how much its heart aches, it falls silent. Even the sad laments of the desert and the wilderness cease. It sighs three times, then falls silent, then sighs thrice more. But mostly it is silent. What it is it does not say, it does not complain, it blames no one, it sighs and once more falls silent. It is as though the silence might cause it to explode, that is why it has to sigh, in order to be silent. The bird is not exempt from suffering, but the silent bird exempts itself thereby from what makes suffering harder to bear, the misunderstanding participation of others; for what makes suffering long-lasting, all the talk of suffering; for what makes suffering into something worse than suffering, the sins of sorrowing and impatience. And don't imagine that this is some kind of false modesty on the part of the bird, that though it might fall silent in the presence of others when suffering it is not, deep within itself, silent but instead laments its state, blaming God and other people . . . No, the bird falls silent and suffers. Ah, but people don't. Then why is it that human suffering seems so terrible by comparison with that of the bird? Is it not, perhaps, because the human can speak? No, that's not the reason – that's actually an advantage. The reason is that the human is unable to fall silent. Matters are not as the impatient or – even more vociferously, the despairing – seem to think when they shout out: 'If only I had a voice like the storm's so that I could express all my suffering just exactly as I experience it!' Alas, that would be a poor resource that would lead only to a proportionately amplified experience of suffering. No, because if you could be silent, if you could emulate the silence of the bird, then your suffering would be less.

And the lily, like the bird, is silent too. It remains silent as it stands and withers. Innocent child that it is, it cannot dissemble. Nor is it required to do so, and its good fortune is that it cannot, for the art is purchased at a high price. It cannot dissemble, can do nothing about its changing colour, which might thereby betray what one already knows from the pale fading – that it is suffering. It remains silent. It might like to remain upstanding to hide the fact of its suffering, but it lacks the strength to do so, lacks this power over itself. Its head droops in weariness and the passer-by understands – if, that is, any passer-by has enough empathy even to notice it! – the passer-by understands what this means, it is eloquent enough. But the lily stays silent.

Thus the lily. But then why does human suffering seem so frightful by comparison with that of the lily? Is it not, perhaps, from the fact that it cannot speak? If the lily were able to speak, and if then, alas, like the humans had not learned the art of staying silent, would not its suffering then seem frightful? But the lily stays silent. For the lily, to suffer is to suffer, no more and no less. And only then, when to suffer is no more and no less than to suffer, is suffering simplified and particularized and kept as small as possible. For suffering cannot be less, since it exists, and is what it is exactly. But suffering that is no longer precisely what it is, no more and no less, can become infinitely greater. When the suffering is neither more nor less than exactly what it is then this makes it finite. No matter that the suffering be great, it is the least that it can be. But when the extent of the suffering lacks such precision then the suffering is much greater, precisely because of the lack of precision. And this lack of precision arises precisely from the ambivalent gift of human speech. A suffering that is precise, on the other hand, in being neither more nor less than it is, can only be attained through knowing how to stay silent. This silence is something you can learn from the bird and the lily.

(*The Lily in the Field and the Bird of the Air*, 1849)

Unsurprisingly, one of Kierkegaard's Old Testament heroes was Job, whose experiences of suffering and whose responses to it continued to fascinate and instruct him throughout his life. Like so many of his suggestions, this idea of bearing our troubles in silence is hard to live out, flying as it does in the face of so much conventional psychological wisdom, from the Catholic confessional to the psychiatrist's couch to the old homily about a trouble shared being a trouble halved. Most of us in any case are unwilling to forgo the simple human comfort of unburdening ourselves to someone we trust when we're having a hard time bearing trouble alone. But complaint can become a habit of mind, and if all we learn from Kierkegaard here is the importance of remembering that discomfort is not the same thing as suffering, and that no one likes a moaner anyway, then that might be the most we can hope for.

7

HOW TO DEAL
WITH DESPAIR

....

The theme of a lot of self-help books is the power of positive thinking; we're told we shouldn't give in to negativity, or pessimism, or despair. Anyone coming from a world in which relentless positivity and optimism are worshipped as the key to a good life will be in for a big surprise if they turn to Kierkegaard to see what he has to say on the subject – and in particular his bewildering enthusiasm for *despair*. Most of us have times when it seems like the end of the world for us, and in that sort of bleak state it's actually quite hard to be told to 'think positively', 'pull your socks up', 'go out and meet people' and so on. Advice like that is easy to give and it looks promising on the printed page; but in the real world of real despair it rarely has the power to change anything.

So how should we deal with despair? Should we try to fight it? Start drinking and hope it's gone by the time we stop? Pretend it isn't there? Run from it?

Or should we turn around and hold out our arms and embrace it?

Amazingly, that's what Kierkegaard advises us to do. Like so much of his advice, what he tries to teach us sometimes seems very strange indeed: why would anyone want to *embrace* despair? So it's important to realize that Kierkegaard uses language and words in a special and personal way. He writes almost like a poet, in the sense that you have to look behind the apparent meaning to get at the deeper one hidden inside it. One of his great ideas was that this Socratic approach was the best way of getting us to understand not only him but ourselves too. It's another aspect of the 'indirect communication' we came across earlier, this time involving a technique that requires you to pretend to know less than you do, even pretend to know nothing at all as you go about searching for answers to your questions. Kierkegaard adds paradox and irony and hyperbole to the mix, until we don't know whether we're coming or going – all we know is that he has something important on his mind, and sooner or later he'll tell us what it is:

> What is to come? What will the future bring? I don't know. Have no idea. When a spider, following its nature, spins down from a fixed point it sees always before it only an empty space in which it can find no hold, no matter how wildly it whirls. It's the same for me: always an empty space in front of me, with the cause that moves me onward lying somewhere

behind me. This life is back to front. It's terrible, unendurable.

... No one comes back from the dead, no one has come into the world without crying. No one asks when you want to enter the world, no one asks when you want to leave ... How empty and meaningless life is. We bury a person; follow him to the grave, throw three shovels of dirt over him. We drive out in a coach and drive back in a coach, and console ourselves with the thought of our own long lives. But really, how long is three score and ten? Why not just get it over with straight away? Why not stay out there, hop down into the grave ourselves and draw lots to see who has the bad luck to be the last one alive, the one to throw the last three shovels of dirt over the last dead person?

(*Either/Or*, 1843)

In *The Sickness unto Death* Kierkegaard provides his own very surprising answer to the question of why not just die and be done with it:

What matters is this: that for God, everything is possible. This is as true for all eternity as it is for each passing moment. It's the sort of thing one says in everyday conversation, an everyday kind of phrase. The truth of it does not emerge until a person has been tested to the uttermost, to the point at which, humanly speaking, possibility no longer exists. Only then does it matter, for one who truly wants to believe, that for God, everything is possible. But this is in fact the formula for losing one's mind: to have faith is to lose your mind and to win God. Think of a person who, with all the shuddering powers of imagination at his disposal, imagines some fearful situation or other which he knows, beyond any shadow of a doubt, he would find unendurable. And one day such a situation arises. In human terms, nothing is more certain than his ruination. The despair in his soul fights desperately to be allowed to despair, for the peace, one might almost say, in which to despair, for the whole of his personality to accept and to give in to despair. There is nothing and no one that a person in such a state would curse more than someone who tried to prevent him from despairing.

. . . Salvation, then, is, humanly speaking, the greatest of all impossibilities. But for God, everything is possible! This is the struggle of faith as it fights insanely, one might say, for possibility, for the only salvation is possibility. When someone faints the cry is for Water, Eau de Cologne, Hoffmann's drops; and when someone is on the verge of despair it is: get me possibility, get me possibility, possibility is the only thing that can save me. A possibility, and the despairing one starts breathing again, he starts living again. Because, without possibility, it is as though a person cannot breathe.

(*The Sickness unto Death*, 1849)

The saving grace of possibility is so closely associated with the idea of God that sometimes, reading Kierkegaard, you feel as if 'possibility' is actually his definition of God:

Sometimes the human imagination will be enough to open up a possibility, but in the end, when it comes to a question of faith, the only thing that helps is that for God everything is possible. So this is the nature of the struggle. Whether or not the struggler goes under depends entirely on whether he is able to get hold of possibility – in other words, if he will believe. And yet he understands that, in human terms, nothing is more certain than his ruination ... The foolhardy person rushes headlong into a danger that contains various possibilities, and if it doesn't work out for him he is finished. The person who has faith sees and realizes to the full his ruination (in terms of what has happened to him, or of the risk he has taken), but still he believes, and for this reason he is not ruined. The way in which he is to be helped is something he leaves up to God, and he believes that, for God, everything is possible. To believe in his own ruination is an impossibility; to believe that his humanity is his ruination, and yet still believe in possibility – that is what it means to have faith. And God does indeed help him, perhaps by sheltering him from fear, perhaps by exposing him to fear: here, unexpectedly and miraculously, divinely, help is at hand ... Whether a person has been miraculously helped depends firstly on the passionate certainty with which he knew that help was impossible; and secondly on how honest he is in his attitude towards the power that did, ultimately, help him. But most, under normal circumstances, do neither one nor the other. They cry out that help is impossible, without even having exercised their own powers of understanding in the search for help; and then afterwards they lie ungratefully.

The believer is in possession of the eternally certain antidote to despair: possibility. Because for God, everything is possible at every moment. This is the truth of faith in which all contradiction dissolves.

(*The Sickness unto Death*, 1849)

Over the last 200 years or so we have turned rationalism into something not far off a religion itself, and it would be very easy for us to turn a deaf ear to Kierkegaard's insistence that all this has something to do with God. But it's worth noting that, particularly towards the end of his life, Kierkegaard was in all-out rebellion against the established Church in his native Denmark.

His passionate insistence on 'inwardness' and taking individual responsibility for our own spiritual lives is actually quite close to the kind of 'personal Christianity' that appeals to many people today. He was so passionate about wanting us to think for ourselves that he toyed with the idea of doing without the Bible altogether:

> Essentially, a Reformation that removed the Bible would have as much validity as Luther's removal of the Pope. All this concentration on the Bible has given rise to the religiosity of learning and theological hair-splitting – a mere entertainment. A degree of learning in such matters has, over time, percolated down to the very lowest levels of society, so that now no one reads the Bible in a human fashion any more. And this does irreparable harm. This attitude has become a refuge for excuses and evasions etc. on the subject of what it means to exist. Because there is always something one has to check on first, always this pretence that the learning must be in place first before one can start to live. Which means, of course, that one never gets round to starting.
>
> (*Papers and Journals 1833–1855*, published posthumously)

Kierkegaard so disliked the idea of anyone – himself included – putting themselves up as experts in spiritual matters (especially priests and bishops, who took money for it) that he always insisted his books were written 'without authority', and even used the phrase as the title of one of them:

What happens in life is like what happened to me when I went to see my doctor. I told him I was feeling ill, and he replied: You probably drink too much coffee and you don't walk enough. Three weeks later I go to see him again and say: I really feel quite ill, but it can't be the coffee-drinking this time, because I'm not drinking any coffee, and it can't be the lack of exercise because I spend the whole day walking. To which he replies: Well then, the reason must be that you're not drinking coffee and you're walking too much. So that was it: my feeling unwell was the same on both occasions, but when I drank coffee it was because I was drinking coffee, and when I didn't drink coffee it was because I wasn't drinking coffee. Same with people. All of our earthly life is a kind of illness. If anyone wonders why this should be so, he is first of all asked how he organizes his life. And once he has responded he is told – well there you are, that's the reason. He asks someone else, and the same procedure is repeated. If he gives a completely different reply this time he is still told – well there you are, that's the reason. And the expert departs with an important look on his face, the look of a man who has explained everything;

until he's out of sight around the corner, whereupon he sticks his tail between his legs and steals away. Even if someone gave me ten rix-dollars I wouldn't take it upon myself to explain the riddle of existence. Why should I? If life is a riddle then, in the end, surely the one who proposed the riddle will explain it himself.

(*Concluding Unscientific Postscript to Philosophical Crumbs*, 1846)

Sometimes, reading Kierkegaard, you feel as though his advice on how to handle despair might work just as well if your faith was in Fate rather than in God. The fatalism and acceptance for which he praises the bird and the lily and commends them to us – aren't these actually divine without their knowing it? What Kierkegaard is telling us in the end is that we cannot work our way *rationally* out of real despair. Words and self-help books and psychoanalysis won't do it. What matters is to have faith in life; and never to forget the power of laughter either. In the midst of our despair, whether it be a cloud that seems to hang over our entire life, or some small, private disappointment that we take too seriously, even as we know we are taking it too seriously – we wanted children but didn't get any; we set our heart on a particular woman but she wanted someone else; there was a job we might have done so well, had we only been given the chance – at a certain point, Kierkegaard suggests, we would do well to remember the liberating gift of laughter:

Something wonderful happened to me. I was transported into the Seventh Heaven. All the gods sat there in assembly. By special grace I was granted the favour of a wish. Said Mercury: 'Will you have Youth, or Beauty, or Power, or Longevity, or the most beautiful girl, or any of the other delights we have in our treasure trove? Choose, but you may only choose one thing.' For a moment I was at a loss, and then I addressed the gods in this fashion: 'My most honoured contemporaries, I choose one thing, and that is always to have laughter on my side.' In reply not one of the gods said a single word. Instead they all began to laugh. From this I gathered that my wish had been granted. I learned, too, that the gods had style: it would, after all, have been inappropriate had they answered, in all solemnity: Your wish is hereby granted.

(*Either/Or*, 1843)

8

HOW TO THINK
ABOUT DEATH

....

We've learned how important it was for Kierkegaard to convey the importance of seeing through the ideas about life and society that have been *sold* to us since our birth. This is vital if we are to have any hopes at all of becoming ourselves. We've seen him urge us not to be afraid of the despair that might come at suddenly finding ourselves awake in the middle of his strange new illusionless world, because only once we feel that despair can we start making firm, strong, deep choices about how we want to live our lives. He was aware of the distress the idea of being true to yourself might bring at first, but he was passionately aware of the need to pursue it as a goal. He was so determined to prove the reality of despair that he analysed the special case of the despair that afflicts those of us who don't even know we have a real self, and suppose ourselves to be perfectly content with everything just as it is. It's an assertion he knows will meet with resistance and even hostility, but he is firmly convinced we are all under-achievers in this respect and he wants to help us realize our full potential:

When a person like this appears to be happy, and supposes himself to be happy and yet is all the time, in the light of the truth, unhappy, then it is rare that he wishes to be rescued from his error. On the contrary, he will respond bitterly, and regard the one who does so as his worst enemy. It will seem to him an assault, something not far off murder, if someone so to speak kills his happiness in this way. And why? Because he is completely in thrall to the sensual and the psychosensual. Because he lives within the categories of the sensual, of what is pleasant and what is unpleasant, and pays no mind at all to spirit and truth. It is because he is too sensual to have the courage to dare to be spirit, to endure being spirit. No matter how vain and self-deluding people are, their notion of themselves is usually really quite banal, by which I mean that they have no notion of being spirit, the ultimate to which a person can aspire; but relatively speaking people are, indeed, vain and self-deluding. Imagine a house that consists of basement, ground floor and first floor, with each floor designed to be occupied by people of different classes. Suppose we compare being a human with such a house; the unfortunate and ridiculous truth is that in most cases people prefer to occupy the basement in their own homes. Every human is a psycho-physical synthesis designed as spirit – spirit being the house; yet he prefers to occupy the basement, which is the

> domain of the sensual. Not only does he choose to
> live in the basement, he actually loves it there, so
> much so that he becomes bitterly angry if someone
> suggests he move to a higher floor, which is standing
> there vacant and ready for him.
>
> (*The Sickness unto Death*, 1849)

The criticism is especially interesting when he gets onto the subject of philosophers, and whether or not their lives reflect the systems they spend their lives labouring to create. Actually, since Kierkegaard's time, philosophy has become more and more divorced from ordinary, everyday daily life. It's become an abstract and academic discipline with its own language and conceptions that seems to have little or no relevance to the lives we actually lead. One of the best things about Kierkegaard is also one of the simplest: that even if we don't agree 100 per cent with him, we can at least understand what he's saying. So he had no time for philosophers who regarded their system of thought as being an abstract creation 'over there' somewhere and did not feel in any way bound to reflect it in the way they lived their own lives. Why should he admire them? The way he looked at it, they weren't *themselves*:

> No, being in error is what people fear least. One sees
> astonishing examples of this that illustrate the truth
> of it on a truly monstrous scale. A philosopher creates

a huge building, a system that extends over the whole of existence and of world history etc. If one then turns one's attention to his personal life, one discovers the ridiculous and appalling and astonishing fact that he does not personally inhabit this enormous, vaulted palace but instead lives in the shed next door to it, or in a dog-kennel, or at best in the porter's lodge. And if you allow yourself, by even a single word, to draw his attention to this contradiction he will be offended. After all, being in error is not what he is afraid of. Not as long as he is able to complete his system – which he does with the aid of this error.

So the fact that someone in despair remains in ignorance of his despair is neither here nor there. He is still in despair. If despair is confusion then a man's ignorance of its presence simply adds error to the confusion. The relationship of ignorance to despair is like that of ignorance to fear . . . the fear of the spiritless manifests itself precisely in the spiritless delusion of safety. Yet fear underpins it all, just as despair underpins it all; and when the bewitchment of the senses passes, and life starts to stumble, then despair is immediately revealed as being at the root of all.

(*The Sickness unto Death*, 1849)

Philosophy for Kierkegaard was prescriptive. It should help us to live good lives and die good deaths. In that respect he has more in common with a Taoist philosopher like the Chinese Chuang Tzu than with most of his own Western contemporaries and near-contemporaries. Sometimes his advice on how to live is ironically expressed . . .

> On paper at least, everyone today is such an absolutely tremendous chap that one sometimes finds oneself plagued by worries that are actually quite groundless. An example of this is the risk people run in our time of finding themselves so quickly done with everything that the question of how to fill the remaining time becomes a real problem. One writes on a piece of paper: doubt everything – and with that one has doubted everything. And if one is not even thirty years old then it can become very difficult to fill up the rest of the time – especially for those who have failed to insure against the coming of old age by learning how to play cards.
>
> (*Concluding Unscientific Postscript to Philosophical Crumbs*, 1846)

. . . and sometimes it's devastatingly commonsensical:

> The task of becoming subjective should give a person plenty to do for as long as he lives. So it will not be the good student but the impatient one who is finished with life before life is finished with him.

And such a one has no right to look upon life with contempt but is instead obliged to concede that he has not understood the task of life properly, this task being self-evidently designed to last the length of a life itself . . . To be finished too soon is the greatest of all dangers . . . Actively to restrain the age is not something I have the time for. And any such attempt would probably be no more successful than the passenger on a train who holds onto the seat in front of him in an attempt to stop the train: he identifies himself as part of the age, and yet still he wants to restrain it. No, the only thing to do is get out of the carriage and restrain yourself. And then once you've left the train – and never forgetting that the task is one of restraint, and the temptation to resist that of finishing too soon – then nothing is more certain than that the task will be sufficient to fill a life. And the fault can then never lie in the task itself, for that is precisely its function: to fill a life.

(*Concluding Unscientific Postscript to Philosophical Crumbs*, 1846)

It's all part of his urgent desire to help us remember how important every single moment of life is. Because life does end, and so he urges us to hear the quiet background hum of death throughout our days, not to let it spoil them, but to enrich them with the reminder not to waste them, because they are not endless:

If it is certain, as indeed it is, that death exists; and that with death's decision all else ends; and if it is certain that death itself never offers us any explanation – well then, we must simply do the understanding ourselves, and a serious under- standing goes like this: that if death is night then life is day, and if we cannot work at night then we can work during the day. And so the short, hurried cry of seriousness – like death's short cry – is: do it today. For death in all seriousness energizes as nothing else does. Like nothing else it stimulates to wakefulness. Death causes the sensualist to say: Let us eat and drink, for tomorrow we shall die. But this is an evasive lust for life, the despicable way of things in the world where one lives to eat and drink, not eat and drink to live. In a deeper soul the idea of death might arouse feelings of impotence that will cause his courage to falter; but for the truly serious person the idea of death gives just the right pace to life, and the right direction in which to use this pace. No bowstring, tensioned to give the arrow pace, can match the pace brought to the living by the thought of death when it has been properly tensioned in seri- ousness. For it is then that seriousness, working to the limits of its powers, takes hold of the matters of the day. No task is too trivial for it nor space of time too short – though it might smile to itself if the whole is said to be to the greater glory of God, and in all impotence and humility be willing to concede that man is nothing at all, and that a man working to the very limits of his abilities earns only the opportunity to wonder at God ... So let death keep its power – 'that it's all over' – but let life keep its right to work while it is still day, and let the serious among us seek help in this from the thought of death.

(*Three Discourses on Imagined Occasions*, 1845)

CONCLUSION:
CHOOSING TO CHOOSE

....

The life of a great thinker or writer or painter has always been important to me in trying to understand that person and get the most out of them. The circumstances of Kierkegaard's life seem to give a tremendous authority to his work for two reasons. I believe him when he says he abandoned the Christian faith of his childhood before regaining it as an adult; and the early deaths in his immediate family – the five dead brothers and sisters, the mother – along with the knowledge that he was physically frail, gave him a uniquely strong sense of death as being something that might come to him at any time. It gave him a vivid sense of the incredible brevity of life. A friend remembered how he was so convinced he wouldn't reach thirty-four that when he did he went to check the date of his birth in the church records, just to make sure.

Kierkegaard is often seen as the father of existentialism, the philosophy associated with Jean-Paul Sartre and Albert Camus that came to prominence in Europe and America in the 1950s. In this sense he was a modern man with a modern mind. He had the kind of agile and large intelligence that sees that every potential course of action and every judgement we make will have something to say for it. The point of view is sometimes known as 'judicial vision', the ability to see both sides (and more) of an argument.

It might be a wonderful talent in a court of law, but in our personal lives, if we are not careful, it can easily tip over into a moral relativism: we say it's all right for someone to rob a bank because they have no money and can't get a job. Or maybe not that it's all right or acceptable, but that at least we *understand* it. And perhaps there *is* something to be said for this point of view (you see the way this works . . .). But to be persuaded of the validity of the other person's point of view all the time can quickly lead to a state of affairs in which we no longer know what we believe, or indeed whether we believe anything at all. In the 1990s television series *The Fast Show*, Paul Whitehouse created a character called Dave. Whenever a discussion or debate arose in the pub this Dave would always agree passionately with whatever the person he was talking to had just said, even when it flatly contradicted something he had already strongly asserted himself. The main character in Woody Allen's film *Zelig* suffered from the same kind of 'chameleonism', this inability to be a self and stick to it. When Groucho Marx took his cigar out of his mouth and boasted: 'Those are my principles and if you don't like them, well, I have others', he was capturing perfectly the hollowness and futility of this dilemma.

Comedians play the failing for laughs, but in our own lives it doesn't always seem that funny. It is just as likely to be a genuine and distressing failure to know where we really do stand on some issue – moral, political, or intellectual – because we have thought about it so much we have orbited all the way round it without ever making our own landing.

In our complex world this is a peculiarly modern problem. So much suffering, so many voices, so many choices – how can we ever know what we think? How can we ever act when the choices never stop coming?

Kierkegaard saw that if every decision and every response is equally valid then, in the end, it really doesn't matter what we decide. In fact, nothing really matters – how can it?

In all its simplicity, this dilemma is a kind of a circular hell. Kierkegaard realized that the best possible escape from it is to have the courage to make your choice, examine it thoroughly and test it out. If it survives, stick to it. Because now it is *your* choice.

The choice Kierkegaard himself made was to step out of the word-driven world of rationalism and take a 'leap of faith' into the irrational world of religion. But he was not a preacher, and he did not urge the same solution on everyone. He believed in passion. For him it was better to hold a mistaken belief passionately than a correct belief insipidly, and in the context of his own Danish society he had more respect for the passionate atheist than for those who made life easy for themselves by their passive acceptance of the state Church's version of Christianity:

> It would indeed be strange were my insignificant person to succeed in something not even Christianity has managed – in evoking passion in the speculative thinker. And if that should happen, well then, suddenly my little crumb of philosophy would acquire a significance of which I could hardly have dreamed. But the person who is neither cold nor hot is an abomination, and God is no more served by such blank individualities than is a rifleman by a gun that clicks at the crucial moment instead of firing.
>
> (*Concluding Unscientific Postscript to Philosophical Crumbs*, 1846)

There are moments when we all realize we've forgotten to remember what an amazing thing it is just to be alive and a thinking human being, and to wonder who we are, and why we're here, and where we're all headed. At times like these it's especially good for me to read Kierkegaard. And it's good for me to read him when things have gone wrong and I've fallen into the trap of blaming God, or other people, or life itself. Then he'll remind me of the fact that I exist myself, for good or ill, and that in the final analysis it is this choice that lies behind any passing disappointment I might suffer. Blaming God or other people doesn't help at all. All you can do is be thankful you've been given a life at all, and then buckle down and try again.

On any objective analysis Kierkegaard's life was not a happy one: the quick, cruel disappearance of that large family; the brief and tormented attempt to start a normal life with Regine, whom in his own strange fashion he continued to love until he died; and his own excruciatingly painful death at the age of forty-two. For an orthodox Christian believer with reasonable expectations of some kind of reward for a life of faithful devotion, you might even say such a fate was humiliating. But Kierkegaard was not an orthodox Christian, and through it all he remained true to his beliefs. He even refused to accept the last rites from a priest, insisting instead on the shocking alternative that a layman do the job. In the event, the last rites were never administered at all.

I could never follow Kierkegaard or try to be a 'kierkegaardian'. In too many respects what he believed in is simply too extreme for me. But I never cease to be fascinated by the great whirlwind of questions he raises about the meaning of life, and by the passion with which he advocated the solution he himself chose – to believe that Christ really was the son of God. I read him the same way as I swim in the sea, with no expectation of understanding the vastness of what I'm experiencing, but filled with gratitude and pleasure at being able to understand – and use – the little bit of it I do.

I hope you feel the same way too.

HOMEWORK

1

HOW TO WAKE UP

....

Is much of your own life lived on autopilot? As an experiment one day, try asking yourself these questions every half hour or so: Am I on autopilot right now? Am I alive to what might happen next?

Kierkegaard strongly believed that boredom is one of the most dangerous of human conditions. In the 1970s Bob Geldof's group the Boomtown Rats had a hit song called 'I Don't Like Mondays'. Listen to the song and see how it relates to this belief.

The next stage after the *aesthetic* in Kierkegaard's outline of the stages of life is the *ethical*. But he says that you cannot be born an ethicist, you must learn to be one. Ask yourself: Can one really *learn* to be an ethical person?

Look back to Kierkegaard's description of the aesthete. Do you recognize yourself in this as someone acting the part of himself in life? If you do, has this seemed to you a strength or a weakness?

Read the play or borrow a DVD of Henrik Ibsen's famous drama *A Doll's House* and then consider this question: If waking up in the Kierkegaardian sense means walking out on your life and leaving your family and your home, as Nora Helmer does in the play, does that make it ethically defensible?

2

HOW TO SEE THROUGH THINGS

....

One of the most famous existentialist novels is *The Outsider* by Albert Camus. Read this short novel and see if you can relate it to Kierkegaard's description of how we split ourselves into two: actors playing the part of ourselves; and spectators watching our own performance. Can you see why Kierkegaard is regarded as one of the founders of existentialism?

Witnesses to a violent bank robbery or a great natural disaster often say afterwards that it was 'like a film'. Kierkegaard was fascinated by representations of life in the form of plays or operas. He found them illuminating, but also seductive and dangerous. Consider the entertainments of our own sophisticated age: is it possible that so much virtual reality and so many reality shows might ultimately create a state of mind in which we find it hard to distinguish between what is real and what is fictional?

Though it might at first seem like a victory for our own independence of mind, Kierkegaard implies that the ability to see through everything can be problematic because we don't know when or how to stop. Listen to Fleetwood Mac's 'Man of the World' and consider this: When the world-weary singer says he wishes he was in love, does he mean he wishes he was in love *again* (because that has always solved his existential problem in the past); or does he mean he has finally seen through the game and realized that he has never really been in love at all?

3

HOW TO AVOID LIVING IN THE PAST

....

Kierkegaard seems to imply that we use the past to create a feeling of comfort and familiarity. Ask yourself: Is he saying that this is another way of falling asleep?

Read Vladimir Nabokov's short novel *Transparent Things*, in which a widower attempts to deal with his grief by revisiting the town and the hotel and even the very room in which he and his late wife spent their honeymoon. Consider this: Do his experiences bear out Kierkegaard's dismissal of the possibility of recreating past happiness in this way?

One of the great confessional novels of the world, Marcel Proust's *In Search of Lost Times*, might seem essentially a hymn in praise of the past. The same could be said of other great autobiographical works, like Rousseau's *Confessions*. So what personal value do these writers derive from delving into their own pasts like this, and what do you think is the value of their work to us?

4

WHY WE SHOULD CULTIVATE DISSATISFACTION

....

Listen to Bob Dylan's 'It's Alright Ma, I'm Only Bleeding', in which he sings that if his thought-dreams could be seen, they'd probably put his head in a guillotine. Then read George Orwell's essay 'Inside the Whale'. Note the passage referring to the Spanish Civil War, in which Orwell observes that many of the people in his circle seemed to be afraid of their own thoughts on the subject ('Ought I to be thinking this?'). Like Kierkegaard, he regarded this kind of self-censorship as unhealthy. Ask yourself this question: How often do I find myself censoring my own thoughts?

If the answer is 'quite often', is this because you worry that people wouldn't like you if they knew what you were really thinking? Or is it because in some way you don't agree with yourself?

Most of us know someone who always seems to speak his or her mind, and most of us admire that person for doing so, even if we don't agree with what they have to say. But in the 'Diapsalmata' Kierkegaard had something else interesting to say on the subject of free speech: 'People demand freedom of speech as a compensation for the freedom of thought, which they seldom use.' Does this description apply to your friend?

5

ON NOT THINKING TOO MUCH

....

Have you ever caught yourself using a process of reasoning to justify to yourself not doing something that you 'know' you ought to have done? If the answer is yes, would this incline you to agree with Kierkegaard that reason is a useful tool, but that it has no part to play in spiritual matters or matters of conscience?

Read the book or watch the DVD of *Man on Wire*, about Philippe Petit's high-wire walk between the Twin Towers back in 1974. When Petit eventually stepped off the wire, he was arrested by a New York policeman. Consider: What does this tell us about the times we live in?

6

WHEN TO SAY NOTHING

....

Read the *Tao Te Ching* by Lao Tzu and compare the mood and sentiment of its closing verse with Kierkegaard's evocation of a calm evening, when 'silence rests over the land, and from some far meadow you hear the lowing of cattle, or from a distant farmer's house the homely bark of the dog'. Consider: In their different ways, are Kierkegaard and Lao Tzu offering us what is in essence the same kind of wisdom?

In certain moods we might feel inclined to dismiss this life lesson on the grounds that Kierkegaard was just being sentimental about birds and flowers. Would we also dismiss, on the same grounds, the interpretations/explanations of the natural world offered us by David Attenborough in programmes like *The Living World*? If not, why not?

Kierkegaard's *Repetition* makes frequent reference to the story of Job. Read *Repetition*, and then read the Old Testament 'Book of Job' and ask yourself: Do you share Kierkegaard's interpretation of the story? For a wordless perspective on this lesson in how to understand suffering, listen to Vaughan Williams's composition *Job: A Masque for Dancing*.

7
HOW TO DEAL WITH DESPAIR
....

The last line of Samuel Beckett's novel *The Unnameable* reads: 'I can't go on, I'll go on.' Consider: In writing that novel, was Beckett saying the same thing as Kierkegaard, that being truthful about life's potential for awfulness is the first precondition for enjoying life? Read Vladimir Nabokov's short novel *Despair*. Can you relate the events in it to Kierkegaard's idea of despair? Or is Nabokov's a different kind of despair?

Finally, ask yourself: Is it harder to praise life or complain about it?

8
HOW TO THINK ABOUT DEATH

....

Read Ibsen's play *The Wild Duck*. Consider: Who do you admire most in that play? Is it Gregers Werle, who believes that the truth must always be told no matter what, or the mildly alcoholic Dr Relling, who believes everyone needs a 'life-lie' in order to get through their days?

Also read *Tropic of Cancer* by Henry Miller. Miller writes: 'I have no money, no resources, no hopes. I am the happiest man alive.' In a Kierkegaardian sense, do you think Miller was deluding himself?

Think about Kierkegaard's assertion that if a philosopher's life does not in some important, practical sense reflect his thought then what he thinks has no special claim on our attention. Do you agree?

The Taoism of Chuang Tzu and Lieh Tzu has no gods, but there are many similarities between their way of looking at things and Kierkegaard's, especially in the scepticism with which they view the claims of rationalism. Do you think it's possible to take God out of Kierkegaard's writing and still be able to get something of value out of it?

Finally, ask yourself: Does Kierkegaard's Christianity put you off reading him, or does it make you curious to read more of his writings? If you do find Kierkegaard stimulating and want to read more, then a great place to start is the *Papers and Journals: A Selection* (translated and edited by Alastair Hannay, London, 1996).

ACKNOWLEDGEMENTS

....

Thanks to Juliette Mitchell for the invitation; to Cindy Chan for her encouragement; to Egil Hjelmervik for the jazz and conversations at Herr Nilsen; to Thor Arvid Dyrerud for the two Kierkegaard books and Jan Erik Holst for the Kierkegaard film; and to Nina for always being interested in the things that matter.

TOOLS FOR THINKING

A NEW RANGE OF NOTEBOOKS, PENCILS & CARDS FROM THE SCHOOL OF LIFE

Good thinking requires good tools. To complement our classes, books and therapies, THE SCHOOL OF LIFE now offers a range of stationery products that are both highly useful and stimulating for the eye and mind.

THESCHOOLOFLIFE.COM
TWITTER.COM/SCHOOLOFLIFE

If you enjoyed this book and would like to discover what other great thinkers can teach us about life, you can buy other titles in this series from THE SCHOOL OF LIFE and get access to exclusive content at: www.panmacmillan.com/theschooloflife

You can also buy our How To guides to everyday living:

If you'd like to explore more good ideas for everyday life, THE SCHOOL OF LIFE runs a regular programme of classes, weekends, secular sermons and events in London and other cities around the world. Browse our shop and visit: